Brady The Busy Beaver

By:

Dr. Charles J. Harrison

Illustrated by:

Charles A. Harrison

Dedication

This book is dedicated to Brady George Kevin Callaway who has a kind heart and a helpful spirit.

Love Aiya

2018

Brady Beaver got up one morning wanting to help.

"I want to help," he said to his mom. "What can I do?"

2

"Go out and help your dad," she said.

Brady thought this was a great idea.

4

Brady could not lift big sticks but he could pick up little ones.

6

After a while, he got good at finding sticks and taking them to his dad.

8

Soon he was helping by putting his sticks on the dam all by himself.

10

The bigger the dam got, the more he had to swim, but this was okay because he got better at swimming.

12

The more Brady helped
the more he felt that he
was doing something
important.

94

Now Brady didn't feel as
bored. He felt more in
charge and like a big
beaver.

16

When the dam was done,
without being told,
Brady helped other
beavers cut up branches
to build their houses.

18

When it came time to eat, Brady saw how some beavers were too little or old to catch their own fish, so he helped them out before catching his own.

20

Brady saw how helping others made him feel good.

22

The more that Brady helped, the more he knew what he was good at, liked, and didn't like.

23

24

When Brady kept on
helping other beavers he
discovered that the
most important thing
was to be kind.

26

By being helpful Brady
felt he was part of the
larger beaver tribe.

28

As he became a grown up beaver, his family and friends saw him as a leader.

THE END